PHYSICAL EDUCATION NOTES CLASS 12

HEMANT RAJ

Made with ♥ on the Notion Press Platform
www.notionpress.com

Contents

CHAPTER ONE

MANAGEMENT OF SPORTS EVENTS

Meaning of sports Management :- Sports managment means to anticipate, plan, organize, appoint, direct and control sporting event any

Functions of sporte Events -Management

1. Planning :- It is an intellectual process of thinking in advance about setting of goals. and developing strategies which are required to attain the goals efficiently.

Objectives of planning

i) To Keep control over all activities.
ii) It also helps in keeping a good control in organizing a tournament.
iii) Reduce the chances of mistake.
iv) To promote innovative ideas
v) To provide direction towards the goal
vi) To reduce undue pressure

2. Organizing: -This includes distributing resources and organizing personel in order to achieve the goals established in the planning function.

3. Staffing: - This refers to identifying key staff positions, and to ensuring that the proper talent is serving that specific job duty in order to achieve the aims and objectives of an organization

4. Directing: - Directing personnel is a leadership quality, and includes letting staff know what needs to be done, and also by when.It includes supervision of personnel while simultaneously motivating them.

5. Controlling:- Controlling refers to all the processes that leaders create to monitor success.It involves establishing performance standards, measuring actual performance and comparing them irregularities.

Various Commities and their responsibilities: -

i) Publicity Committee: All the press releases and press conferences are conducted by this committee.
ii) Transport Committee: This committee is responsible for providing the facilities regarding transportation of various teams If the venue of sports events.
iii) Reception Committee: The members of this committee are responsible to welcome the Chief Guest and spectators at opening and closing ceremonies.
iv) Boarding and Lodging Committee: This committee is responsible for making necessary arrangements for providing accommodation and serving meals to the sportspersons and other officials.
v) Ground and Equipment Committee: This committee makes necessary arrangements of equipment related to events.
vi) Medical and First Aid Committee: This committee is Formed to provide medical assistance to participants round the clock
vii) Finance Committee: This committee is assigned to make the budget for the event and handle the expenses.
viii) Refreshment Committee: This committee is formed to provide refreshment to the participants.

Tournament is a series of contests in which a number of contestants compete and the one that prevails through the final round or that finishes with the best record is declared the winner.

Type of tournament:

1. Knock out: In this type of tournament, the team once defeated, gets eliminated from the tournament. Only the winning teams contest in the next rounds. Opportunities are given to the winning players/teams.

2. League: In single league tournament all participating teams compete once, with each other, whereas in double league, each team plays with every as in double league, each team plays with every other team twice, without any consideration of victory or defeat

a) Cyclic method: In cyclic method, If the number of teams is in even number, the team number 1 is fixed on the top of left-hand side and then other team numbers in ascending order consecutively downward and then upward on the left-hand side and then from the next round teams will rotate in clockwise direction. If the number of teams is odd then the bye is fixed on the top of right-hand side and rest of the procedure will remain same. If the number of team is even number than number of rounds will be (N-1). If the number of teams is odd number, then number of rounds will be equal to number of teams.

b) Stair-case Method: In stair-case method, the fixtures are made just like a ladderor a stair- case. In this method, no bye is given to any team and there is no problem of even or odd number of teams.

3. Combination Tournaments: Combination tournaments are organized in group or zonal matches.

There are mainly four types of combination Tournaments...

1.Knock out cum Knock out

2.League cum league

3.Knock out cum league

4.League cum Knock out

Seeding a Team: -The sorting of the teams and fitting them in the fixtures so that the stronger teams do not meet each other in earlier rounds is known as Seeding.

Bye: -The advantage given to a team usually by drawing a lot, and exempting it from playing a match in the first round is known as Bye.

Pre-Tournament Responsibilities: -

i) To prepare the budget of the tournament

ii) To prepare the schedule or programme of the sports tournament

iii) To prepare sports grounds /courts / track, sport equipment.

iv)To arrange prizes and certificates for winners.

v)To send various information about dates and venue to team

vi) to form various committees.

During Tournament Responsibilities: -

i) To ensure proper arrangement during inauguration.

ii) To check the sports ground/field / court and sports equipment.

iii) To check the arrangement of refreshments.

iv) To impart first aid to the injured athletes

v) To maintain proper discipline

vi)To prepare proper Scoresheet for record.

Post Tournament Responsibilities

i) To give away the prizes and certificates to winner

ii) To provide detailed results and other necessary information to the media.

iii) To provide security refund to the departing team.

iv) To make the payments to the officials.

v) To collect all the records/files related to the sports tournament

Advantage of Knock-out tournament

i) The Knock out tournament are less expensive because the teams get defeated, is eliminated from the competition.

ii) The Knock out tournament is helpful in enhancing the standard of sports, because each team tries to give the best performance to avoid defeat
iii) Owing to less number of matches, the tournaments get completed in less time
iv) Minimum number of officials are required in organising such types of Tournaments.

Disadvantages of Knock-out Tournament.
i) There may be many chances of elimination of good teams in the 1st or 2nd round. So, good teams may not reach the final round
ii) There are more chances of weak teams to enter the final round
(iii) Spectors may lose interest in the final match if weak teams reach in final round

Advantage of league tournament: -
i) Only strong or deserving team gets victory in the tournament.
ii) Every team gets maximum opportunities to show its efficiency or performance.
(iii) The Spectors also gets good opportunities to watch the game for many days.
iv) A team need not wait to win against the other team for playing a match

Disadvantages of the league tournament.
i) It requines more time.
ii) It cost more.
iii) It requemes making more arrangement for sports officials and teams.
iv)The teams coming from far and wide generally face more problems because such tournaments waste their time and money.

Meaning of Intramural: -

Intramural is derived from the Latin word 'Intra"and "muralist'."Intra" means "within" and "Muralist" means 'Walls' .So we can say that the activities, which are performed within the walls or within the campus of an institution, are called 'Intramural".

Objectives of Intramural: -
1. To provide opportunity to every student to participate in games and Sports
2. To develop Leadership Qualities among students
3. To develop Feeling of Cooperation
4. To provide Recreation

Extramurals :Extramural sports satisfy the need or structured sports activities between students from various schools, organizations, or institutions. Extramural means competitions outside walls or boundaries, as of a city or town or a university. These tournaments will be organized on a zonal, regional, state or national basis. Eg: CBSE tournaments etc.

Objectives of extramural:
1. To provide Experience to Students
2. To improve the Standard of Sports
3. To broaden the Base of Sports
4. To develop Sportsmanship and Fraternity
5. To provide knowledge of New Rules and Advanced Techniques

Community Sports - Purpose and benefits

Sports and games programs are arranged in the world as well as in our country to promote the games and sports for a specific cause. Every country in the world has some or other cause for promoting Community sports programs. The programs motivate and create the feeling to take part in these sports programs. People become health conscious and try to remain fit and stay healthy for as long as possible. These specific sports programs are usually organized by the federations, state government, NGO etc. to create health consciousness among the people and take part in healthrelated sports programs.More and more people of all age groups should take part in such sports programs. Specific sports programmes are such programmes of sports which are not usually related to competitions. These programmes have various objectives such as creating awareness among peoples regarding unity, health & diseases etc.

The various important specific programs are: -

1. SPORTS DAY

2.HEALTH RUN : These are organized by health departments to Know the standard of health in a country along with raising funds for charity.

3.RUN FOR FUN : It is also organised to spread the message among masses to remain healthy and fit. It may be organized to motivate the people to remain fit.

4.RUN FOR UNITY: It is organized to show unity and peace among the people of different religions. Its purpose may be national and international integration and brotherhood.

5.RUN FOR SPECIFIC CAUSE : This is the run related to specific or noble cause. Most of the social non- profit organizations organizes these runs for creating awareness about AIDS, Educating the girl child, Cancer.

CHAPTER TWO

CHILDREN & WOMEN IN SPORTS

Meaning of motor development

Moter development means the development of various motor abilities from birth till death.

Motor development divided into two types

i) Gross Motor development: - It involves the development of large muscle in the child's body specially while sitting, walking, running etc.

ii) Fine motor development: - It involves the small muscle of the body, especially during the small movement of the finger and handExercise Guidelines of WHO for different age groups

1. Infancy (0-2 years)

A. Exercise to develop head control, sitting & crawling,
B. Gross motor activities should be promoted,
C. Exercise for moving arms, legs, reaching to object,
D. Exercise like throwing, catching & kicking a ball,

2. Early childhood (3 to 6 years)

A. Exercise to develop competence in movement skills.
B. Emphasis on participation not on competition.
C. Activities related to fine motor skills.
D. Minimum one-hour regular medium exercise.
E. Recreative & enjoyable methods of physical activities.
F. Clean & safe environment.

3. Middle child hood (7 to 10 years)

A. Exercise to develop fine & gross motor skills
B. Exercises to build & improve coordination skills
C. Exercises to develop synchronize the movements of body's parts.
D. Introduction of major sports activities cognitive and social skills

4. Later childhood (11 to 12 years)

A. Exercise to develop body control, strength and coordination.
B. Activities related to endurance should be avoided.
C. Organized or team games to develop social consciousness.
D. Teach basic rules of sports i.e., fair, play, simple strategies.
E. Introduction to concept of sport training

5. Adolescence (13 to 18 years)

A. Moderate to vigorous intensity physical activity.
B. 60 min to several hours every day.
C. Muscle strengthening exercise at least 3 times a week.
D. Bone strengthening exercise and resistance exercise by weight training.
E. Running swimming etc. for stamina building.

6. Adult hood (19-60 years)

A. Moderate intensity physical every day.

B. Muscles strengthening exercise at least 2 times a week.
C. Bone strengthening exercise and resistance exercise.
D. Running, swimming, etc. for stamina building

7. Old age (60 years and above)

A. At least 5 days of moderate intensity activities such as walking, light- jump etc. It should be done for above 45- 60 minutes. These actions should be done over a period of 10-10 minutes.
B. Those who are more active than an elderly mature, they should do more than 30 minutes of high-strength activity, combined with the actions of moderate intensity. Such as climbing stairs, running etc.

Common Postural Deformities and their Corrective Measures

Knock Knee - Knock Knees, also known as Genu valgum, is a knee misalignment that turns the knees inward. As a result, both knees touch or knock against each other in a normal standing posture but there is a gap of 3-4 inches between the ankles.

Causes of knock knee:

(i) Weakness of muscles and ligaments
(ii)Overweight body
(iii)Lack of balanced diet
(iv)Lack of vitamin-D

Corrective measures of Knock Knees:

Walking on an outward inclining surface and applying pressure on the outer edge of the feet Exercises like horse riding and keeping the pillow between the knees and standing erect for some times are the best.

Yoga:
1. Padmasana
2. Gomukhasana

Flat Foot:

Flat foot is also known as pes planus or fallen arches. It is a condition that may be diagnosed by looking at the arch of the foot or by taking the water print test. As the name flat foot suggests, people suffering from this deformity have either no arch in their feet, or one that is very low, allowing the entire soles of the feet to touch the floor in standing position.

Causes of Flat foot:

1.Faulty posture
2.Prolonged standing
3.Excessive body weight
4.Lack of proper exercises

Corrective measures of flat foot:
1.Heel and toe Walking
2.Walking on sloping surface

Exercises like jumping on toes and heels, skipping rope, strengthens the muscles of foot which help to develop the arch in the foot.

Activities like picking up marbles with toes, writing numbers in the sand with the toes will also help in developing the arch.

Yoga:
1. Adhomukhasana
2. Vajrasana

Bow Legs:

Bow Legs, also known as Genu varum, is a position of knees in which legs look like a bow, when the legs curve outward at the knees while the feet and ankles touch.Infants and toddlers often have bow legs. It may be caused due to lack of Vitamin D, Phosphorus and Calcium and can be easily cured at an early stage.

Corrective Measures of Bow legs:

Feed calcium to children

Use of braces and modified shoes can be along with sufficient intake of balanced diet can prove to be of help. Walking on the inner edge of the feet may also help.

Round Shoulder:

It is a postural deformity in which the shoulders are drawn, the head is extended with the chin pointing forward.

Causes of round shoulders:

(i) Due to poor posture while working
(ii) Faulty furniture
(iii) Wrong habit of sitting / standing
(iv) Carrying heavy load on shoulders
(V) By sleeping on one side

Corrective measures of Round Shoulders:

1.Regular Exercise
2.Leaning back on the chair

Most important measure to correct rounded shoulders is strengthening and stretching of muscles and trying to correct the imbalance of muscles by doing chest stretches, wall stretch, planks, pull ups, reverse shoulder stretch, etc.

Yoga asanas:

1. Chakrasana
2. Dhanurasana

Kyphosis:

Kyphosis is also known as Hunch Back or round upper back.It is a condition of the spine where the curvature of the upper back gets exaggerated or increases. It is an exaggerated, forward rounding of the back.

Cause of Kyphosis:

1.Habit of holding the head forward in an abnormal manner
2. Kyphosis can occur due to heredity, aging, disease (arthritis, osteoporosis), malnutrition, pulling of heavy weight over a period, unstable furniture, poor postural habit, weakness in muscles etc.

Corrective measures of Kyphosis:

Physical therapy, swimming, exercise/ gym ball exercises, exercises with bands

Yoga asanas:

1. Dhanurasana,
2. Chakrasana
3. Bhujangasana

Lordosis:

It is a common defect in deformity & posture.Here lumber curve becomes more pronounced and front central position of pelvic region is tilted forward

Corrective measures of Lordosis:

Exercises to develop strength in the pelvic region like sit-ups, sitting against the wall and pushing the trunk backward and lying on the back and raising upper extremities and legs together will give significant benefits.

Yoga asanas:

1. Dhanurasana
2. Halasana

Scoliosis-

The word Scoliosis comes from the Greek skolios which means bent. Scoliosis is a position in which the spine is tilted to either side of the body. It is a position of exaggerated lateral curvature or sideways curvature of the spine. In this disorder, the spine bends, twists or rotates in a way that it makes a C or an S shape.

Corrective measures of scoliosis:

In cases of mild Scoliosis, no treatment is necessary. Some children may need to wear a brace to stop the curve from worsening. Others may need surgery to keep the problem from worsening and to straighten the spine. Exercises like hanging on the horizontal bars and swinging should be done on opposite side of the C-shaped curve.

Breaststroke in swimming

Yoga:

1. Trikonasana
2. Adhomukhasana

Sports Participation of Women in India:

Sports Participation of women means women Participation in the field of sports and games.

In 1952 Olympic games, the first India women took part. In 2000 Olympia games, Karnam Malleshwari (weight lifting) become the first Indian women to have won a bronze medal. Special consideration (Menarche & Menstrual Dysfunction) The period of adolescence is marked by certain universal physical and biological changes in the body which lead to the attainment of sexual maturity. The time when sexual maturity is reached is called puberty.

Menarche (first menstruation) is usually considered the point of sexual maturity for girls. It is the process in which female reproduction system matures and the body prepares itself for potential pregnancy.

Special consideration (Menarche & Menstrual Dysfunction)

Menstruation (also termed as period or bleeding) is the process in a woman of discharging (through the vagina) blood and other materials from the lining of the uterus at about a monthly interval from puberty until menopause, except during pregnancy.This discharging process lasts about 3-5 days. Women usually have periods until about ages 45 to 55 and have menopause usually around age of 50.

Menopause means that a woman is no longer ovulating and can no longer get pregnant.

Menstrual dysfunction is an abnormal condition in a woman's menstrual cycle.

Normal range of the menstruation cycle is 21 to 35 days. If it happens earlier than 21 days or after more than 35 days, then it's a problem.Other menstrual problems include missing three or more periods, menstrual flow heavier or lighter in comparison with usual, cycle happening longer than seven days, any pain, cramping or vomiting during period, bleeding after menopause etc.

Causes of abnormal menstrual cycles or menstrual order are:

1. Overweight,
2. Stress,
3. Dietary disorder,
4. Disease,
5. Sudden change in exercise schedule,
6. Travel,
7. Other medical complications etc.

Special consideration (Menarche & Menstrual Dysfunction)

Sports like Judo, boxing, wrestling, taekwondo etc. exert a lot of pressure on athletes to maintain their shape and weight. Participation in sports like distance running, cycling, cross country etc. athletes have to take a balanced diet since these demand high levels of energy and a good quantity of dietary intake.

Such pressures put the athlete's health at risk and leads to Female Athlete Triad. The term 'triad' was first described by American college of sports medicine in 1992, and the three components to describe the triad were Osteoporosis It is weakening of the bone due to the loss of bone density & improper bone formation due to insufficient amount of calcium in skeletons system.

Amenorrhoea is a menstrual disorder or illness in females of 18yrs & above either never begin menstruolispor absence of menstruations for three or more months

OR

The cessation of women's menstrual cycle for more than three months or more Eating disorders These are mental illness which cause disturbances of an individual's regular diet

OR

It is a range of psychological disorder in which a person's eating behavior is abnormal. It may normal. It may include inadequate or excessive food intake which can ultimately harm an individuate wellbeing These types are

a. Anorexia Nervosa b. Bullimia Nervose

CHAPTER THREE

YOGA AS PREVENTIVE MEASURE FOR LIFESTYLE DISEASE

International Yoga Day

Celebrated all over the world on June 21 since its inception in 2015. The idea of IDY was first proposed by Prime Minister Narendra Modi during his speech at the United Nations General Assembly (UNGA), on September 27, 2014.The date of June 21 was suggested by PM Modi in his UN address as it is the longest day of the year in the Northern Hemisphere and is highly important in many parts of the world.

YOGA

The term yoga is derived form a Sanskrit word 'Yuj' which means join or union. In fact, joining the individual self with the divine or universal spirit is called yoga. It is a science of development of man's Consciousness.

Elements of Yoga:

The main aim of yoga is to control over the mind.This is Possible only follow to eight-fold Paths or eight steps also known as "Ashtang Yoga". This system was Developed by Maharashi Patanjali.

Obesity

Obesity is that condition of the body in which the amount of fat increases to extreme levels. Now A days obesity has become a problem for the whole world obesity is a condition in which the amount of fat in the body increase to a very large extent.

If a person is having BMI > 30 he/she would be considered as obese.

There are many causes of obesity such as

•Overeating,

•Lack of physical exercise,

•Genetics,

•Diet high in carbohydrate

•High frequency of eating,

•Medications,

•Psychological factors.

Due to many health risks of obesity, it has been given the status of a disease. Due to obesity, diseases like Diabetes,High blood pressure,Cancer,Arthritis etc. are caused.

Benefits:

a) It is helpful for concentration.

b) It is helpful in curing back pain and chest diseases.

c) It enhances memory.

d) It cures problems related to menstruation.

e) It cures mental stress.

f) It removes postural defects.

Contraindications:

a) A person suffering from joint pain should not perform vajrasana.

b) The individuals who have any spinal column problem should not perform this asana.

c) The individuals who have some difficulty in movement should practice this asana with a lot of care
Tadasana, Katichakrasana, Pavanmuktasana, Matsayasana, Halasana, Pachimottansana, Ardha Matsyendrasana, Dhanurasana, Ushtrasana, Suryabedhan pranayama

Diabetes

Diabetes is such a disorder that it causes sugar to build up in our blood stream instead of being used by the cells in the body.Diabetes is commonly known as metabolic disorder characterized by high blood sugar level over a prolonged period. Diabetes is due to either the pancreas not producing enough insulin or the cells of the body not responding

Symptoms of Diabetes
'Fatigue
'Increased Thirst
'Increased Hungers
'Blurred Vision
'Kidney Failure
'Cardio vascular Disease
'Loss of Weight
'Frequent Urination
Causes of Diabetes
'Sedentary life stages
'Disease
'Over weight
'Obesity
'Stress & Tension

Types of Diabetes:

(a) Type I Diabetes: In that type of diabetes blood sugar level rises very high due to non-secretion of insulin hormone by pancreas. In that of diabetes effected person has to take artificial insulin through injection.

(b) Type II Diabetes: In that type of diabetes blood sugar level rises but not as such as high in type I diabetes. In that type of diabetes our pancreas secreting the insulin hormone but it may be insufficient to control the blood sugar level normal or body cell are not able to respond insulin properly.

Katichakrasana, Pavanmuktasana,Bhujangasana, Shalabhasana, Dhanurasana, Supta-vajarasana, Paschimottanasana, ArdhaMastendrasana, Mandukasana, Gomukasana, Yogmudra, Ushtrasana, Kapalabhati;

Asthma

Asthma is a disease of lungs in which the airways become blocked or narrowed causing difficulty in breathing.The airways also swell up. It usually triggers coughing, wheezing or whistling or shortness of breath.

Common symptoms of asthma are:
coughing,heavy breathing,chest tightness,fatigue,pain in hands, feet, shoulders and back.
Reasons are dust, smoke, air pollution, pollen grains, animals' skin, hair or
feather etc. are the main reasons

Tadasana, Urdhwahastottansana, Uttan Mandukasana, Bhujangasana, Dhanurasana, Ushtrasana, Vakrasana, Kapalbhati, Gomukhasana Matsyaasana, Anuloma-Viloma

Hypertension:

Hypertension is another name for high blood pressure.It can lead to severe complications and increases the risk of heart disease, stroke, and death.

High blood pressure:

A condition in which the strength of blood against the walls of the artery is very high.
Reasons for high blood pressure increased with age, Genetic, obesity, lack of physical activity, smoking, alcohol, more intake of salt in food, tension or mental stress, diabetes, pregnant women are more prone to high B.P. All these factors

can lead to high blood pressure.

The main function of the heart is to supply pure blood to the various parts of the body through different arteries when the heart contract it pushes the blood through blood vessels and consequently, the blood pressure increases in arteries this pressure is known as Systolic blood pressure. It is represented by the first number the pressure between two heartbeats is called Diastolic blood pressure. It is represented by bottom or second number these two numbers of blood pressure are measured in mm/Hg. Unit is millimeter of mercury. The normal blood pressure of an adult is considered 120/80mm/Hg.

The person whose blood pressure readings are beyond 140/90 mm/Hg are said to be having hypertension.

Tadasana, Katichakransan, Uttanpadasana, Ardha Halasana, Sarala Matyasana, Gomukhasana, UttanMandukasana, Vakrasana, Bhujangasana, Makarasana, Shavasana, Nadi-shodhanapranayam, Sitlipranayam

Back pain

It is the pain felt in the backbone. Episodes of back pain may be acute, sub- acute, or chronic depending on the duration. The pain may be characterized as a dull ache, shooting or a burning sensation. The pain may originate from the muscles, nerves, bones, joints. It is generally caused by strained muscles, ruptured disk, sciatica, arthritis, osteoporosis, abnormal curvature of spine, cancer of the spine, etc.

Causes of back pain

(a) Over weight

(b)Lack of exercise

(c) Bad Sitting/ sleeping posture

(d)Lack of Flexibility.

(e) Undue Stress on back

(f) Improper warming up and cooling

Tadasana, Urdhawahastottansana, Ardha-Chakrasana, Ushtrasana, Vakrasana, Sarala Matsyendrasana, Bhujangasana, Gomukhasana, Bhadrasana, Makarasana, Nadi-Shodhana Pranayam;

CHAPTER FOUR

PHYSICAL EDUCATION & SPORTS FOR CWSN

Disability:- Any disadvantage due to which an individual is not able to perform the activities of normal human life is known as disabilitiesAll persons with all types of disabilities must enjoy all human rights and fundamental freedoms. To give the effect to the United Nations Convention on the Rights of Persons with Disabilities an act names the Rights of Persons with Disabilities Act 2016 (RPWD Act 2016) was passed by Indian Parliament on 27th December 2016.

Concept of Disorder:

Disorder is usually used for mental disabilities. Disorder is any ailment that disturbs the health of an individual. Disorder creates hindrance in an individual's performance and reduces his efficiency. In the beginning disorder seems to be ordinary but they usually grow or spread in a harmful manner in an individual.

It is a matter of confusion for many as to what is the right term – Disability/Disorder/Children with Special Needs/ Divyanga.

As per the Disability Act 2016, "Person with Disability" or Divyangjan are the acceptable terms.

Disorders are used frequently in medical terminology whereas Children with Special Needs (CWSN) is more frequent in educational set up.

Organizations promoting adaptive sports

1. Special Olympic:

Special Olympics is the world's largest sports organization for children and adults with intellectual disabilities and physical disabilities, providing year- round training and activities to 5 million participants and 172 countries.

Special Olympics competitions are held every day, all around the world including local, national and regional competitions, adding up to more than 100,000 events a year.

The Special Olympics World Games is a major event put on by the Special Olympics committee.

The World Games alternate between summer and winter games, in two- year cycles, recurring every fourth year. The first games were held on July 20, 1968, in Chicago.

2.Para Olympics:

This is similar to Olympic game for disabled sports person.In 1960 first time it was organized in Rome. The head quarter of international para-Olympic is situated at Bonn, Germany.The international para-Olympic is responsible for organizing summer and winter Olympic games. At present it comprises of 176 National Para Olympic Committees.

India at Para Olympics:

India made its Summer Paralympic debut at the 1968 Games, competed again in 1972, and then was absent until the 1984 Games. The country has participated in every edition of the summer games since then. It has never participated in the Winter Paralympic Games.India's first medal in Paralympics came in 1974 Games, with Murlikant Petkar winning a gold medal in swimming. India's best finish yet has been

in the 2020 Games, at 24th place with a medal haul of 19 medals (5 gold, 8 silver and 6 bronze).

3. Deaflympics:

The 'Deaflympics' are games for deaf athletes. Previously they were called the international games for the Deaf. These games are organized by "The International committee of sports for the Deaf" since the first event and they are sanctioned by International Olympic committee.

The deaf Olympian cannot be guided by sounds for example, the starter gun, bullhorn commands or refree whistles. The Deaflympics were held in Paris in 1924 and were also the first ever international sporting events for athletes with disability.

The Deaflympic winter games, was added in 1949. The games began as a small gathering of 148 athletes. Now these games are grown into a global movement. To qualify for the games, athletes must have a hearing loss of at least 55db in their "better ear".Hearing aids, cochlear implant is not allowed to be used in competition.Deaflympics cannot be guided by sounds so alternative methods are used to address the athletes. For example, the football referees wave a flag instead of blowing a whistle, on the track races are started by using a light, instead of using a starting pistol.

Need of Inclusion:

Inclusion in physical education helps the students with disabilities to increase their social skills and in making friends.A child feels that he/she also belongs to the entire group of class so a feeling of belongingness is developed.Inclusion helps a child to increase his/her motor skills and experience success with peers.

Inclusion Implementation:

To make inclusion work, general classroom teachers, support specialist, parents and students themselves must work together to create the best educational environment possible.

With knowledge of inclusive practices and strategies, teachers can manage, classrooms that encourage learning and discovery among all students, regardless of physical abilities.

School principals must cooperate and share the message that all staff members, not just special education teachers, all of them are expected to be involved in education children with disabilities.

Inclusion also requires specially trained staff. Since classroom teachers need training and ongoing support to effectively teach many types of learners, they must meet regularly with inclusion specialists.

School Counselor

Special education counsellors work with special need children in elementary school, middle schools and high schools to ensure they have the support services they need in order to achieve their highest potential in the areas of academics, personal and social and career development.

Occupational Therapist

The goods of occupational therapy for a child are to improve participation and performance of a child and all the child's "occupation" like self-care, play, school and other daily activities.The occupational therapist well assesses the child and modify the environment, or the way of doing a task to promote a better participation and independence.

Physical Education Teacher

Physical education program plays a very progressive role in improving cognitive functions and academic performance. Social skills and collaborative team work can also be enhanced through the different programs of physical education. The physical education teacher helps in executing these programs.

Physiotherapist:

Physiotherapist the best-known therapist who work with children with special needs.They use exercises to help their patients and keep the best possible use of their bodies. They also try to improve breathing to prevent the development of deformities and to slowdown the deterioration caused by some progressive diseases.

Speech Therapist:

Speech therapist is known by many names like speech language pathologist, speech pathologist and speech teacher.They work with children with a variety of delays and disorders spanning from mild articulation delays to more complex disorders such as autism, down syndromes, hearing impairment, motor speech disorders and other developmental delays. Speech teacher helps your child with speech, talking and communication.

Special Education Teacher:

Special education teachers work in classrooms or resource centers that only include students with disabilities.Students with disability may attend classes with general education students also known as inclusive classrooms. special education teacher's duties vary by the type of setting they work in, student disabilities and teacher specialty

Advantages of Physical Activities for children with special needs.

1. To build a Programme to meet the needs of CWSN
2. To build in CWSN the capacity to be functionally active for lifetime
3. To provide a safe and accessible PE and sports Programme as per the needs of the individual
4. To ensure active participation or transition towards the integrated or regular PE Programme (Inclusion)
5. Helping to develop self-esteem in CWSN
6. To promote regularity and discipline
7. To promote sportsmanship

Strategies to make physical activities accessible for children with special needs

a) medical check-up:

If we want to make physical activities accessible for the CWSN, we need to understand the type of disabilities of children and for this purpose complete medical check-up of the children is required. Because without complete medical check-up of the children is required. Because without complete medical check-up, the teachers of physical education cannot come to know about the type of disability child is facing

b) Activities based on interests:

Physical activities must be based on interest, aptitudes, abilities, previous experience and limitations of children with special needs experience and limitations of children with special needs.

c) Different instructional strategies:

A variety of different instructional strategies such as verbal, visual and peer teaching should be used for performing various types of physical activities. By these children get opportunity to learn by their own and become independent.

d) Modification of rules:

Rules can be modified according to the needs of the children. They can be provided extra time or attempt to perform a physical activity.

e) Specific environment:

For special needs children the area should be limited. In case of children who have autism, they must be provided specific area because they may need some time to relax.

CHAPTER FIVE

SPORTS AND NUTRITION

Balanced Diet: - A diet which contains the proper amount of each nutrient, i.e., like carbohydrate, fat, protein etc. according to the needs of individual is called Balanced Diet.

OR

A diet which consists of all the essential food constituents i.e protein, carbohydrates, fats, vitamins, minerals and water in correct proportion is called balanced diet.

Nutrition: - It is the process of obtaining & consuming food or breaking down food & substances taken in by the mouth to use for energy in the body.

Nutrients: - The energic food in our diet consists of various types of essential chemicals for our body termed as nutrients: - e.g. Protein, fat, carbohydrates, vitamins & minerals.

Goals of nutrition:

(i) stay hydrated
(ii) provide immediate fuel
(iìí) boost performance
(ív) preserve muscle and
(v) improve recovery.

Macro nutrients:

Macronutrients mainly include carbohydrates, proteins and fats and also water which are required in large quantities and their main function being the release of energy in body. Ex: Macronutrients include Carbon, Oxygen, Hydrogen, and Nitrogen. Carbohydrates, proteins and fats are macronutrients and are also called 'Proximate principles' because they form the main bulk of the diet.

In Indian meals, they contribute to the total energy intake in the following proportion: carbohydrates: 55-60%; protein: 10-15% and fats: 20-30%. Water does not provide energy but is a vital nutrient required in large quantity for functioning of metabolic processes in the body and various regulatory functions. Therefore, it is also considered a macronutrient. Micro nutrients: Micronutrients mainly comprise vitamins and minerals which are required in minute quantities. However, both macro nutrients as well as micro nutrients are essential. Ex: Micro nutrients are chlorine, iron, manganese, zinc,boron, sodium, copper, molybdenum and nickel.

Non-Nutritive and Nutritive Components of Diet

Nutritive components of diet:

CARBOHYDRATES –

Carbohydrates are organic compounds made up of Carbon, Hydrogen and Oxygen.
Carbohydrates are a major source of energy and provide 4kcal per gram.
Carbohydrates are needed to provide energy during exercise.
Carbohydrates are stored mostly in the muscles and liver. Complex
carbohydrates are found in foods such as pasta, bagels, whole grain breads, and rice

PROTEIN –

Protein is important for muscle growth and to repair body tissues. Protein can also be used by the body for energy, but only after carbohydrate stores have been used up.

Only strength training and exercise will change muscle. Athletes, even body builders, need only a little bit of extra protein to support muscle growth.

Athletes can easily meet this increased need by eating more total calories (eating more food).

Protein requirement for Indian adults is 1 g/kg body weight (according to ICMR).Thus, for a man weighing 60 kg, the protein requirement would be 60g/day. In terms of percentage of total energy intake, protein intake should be between 10-15% of total energy consumed.

In no case, it should exceed 35% of total energy intake. Protein requirement,however, may increase to up to 2 g/ kg body weight during sports and exercise depending upon the type of sports and duration and

intensity of training.Too little, or, excess intake of protein has health implications, hence proteins should be consumed as required and recommended.

Fat: -

It provides the highest concentration of energy of all the nutrients. One gram of fat equals nine calories. One pound of stored fat provides approximately 3,600 calories of energy.Saturated fats are found primarily in animal sources like meat, egg yolks, yogurt, cheese, butter, milk. This type of fat is often solid at room temperature. Unsaturated fats include monounsaturated and polyunsaturated fats, which are typically found in plant food sources and are usually liquid at room temperature.

Vitamin –

A well-planned and nutritionally adequate diet should meet an athlete's vitamin and mineral needs. will only be of any benefit if your diet is inadequate or you have a diagnosed deficiency, such as an iron or calcium deficiency.

Use of vitamin and mineral supplements is potentially dangerous and they should not be taken without the advice of a qualified health professional.

Minerals: -

Mineral are very essential in our diet. 4% of our body weight is made up of minerals. These are required for healthy teeth, bones and muscles.

It is also used by body for various activities such as transmission of nerve impulses, formation of hormones and maintenance of heart beat etc.

Macro Minerals: -

a) Calcium: Calcium is among the top macrominerals in terms of growth and development of our bones and teeth. It helps in blood clotting.Its deficiency may cause rickets. The sources are cheese, milk, orange, juice, eggs, green leafy vegetables and cereals.

b) Potassium: Potassium is one of the most required minerals in diet. It is helpful in keeping the nervous system and muscular system fit and active all the time.

It helps in maintaining the amount of water in blood and tissues. Its main sources are banana, tomatoes, green leafy vegetables, beans etc.

c) Sodium: It helps in muscular activities. It also helps in transmission of nerve impulses.The sources are table salts, pickles and butter etc.

d) Magnesium: It repairs and maintains body cells. It is found in meat, brown rice, beans and whole grains etc.

e) Phosphorus: Phosphorus helps in the formation of bone and teeth. It keeps the muscles and nerve activities normal.The sources are egg, fish, liver, milk, and unpolished rice etc.

Micro Minerals:

a) Iodine: It produces the hormones for the thyroid gland. It is also significant for proper growth and development.Lack of iodine can cause goiter (swollen thyroid gland) and mental retardation. The sources iodized salt, fish and sea food.

b) Iron: It is essential in the production of hemoglobin. Its deficiency causes anemia. The sources are meat, egg, dry fruits, spinach banana and greet leaf vegetables.

c) Chromium: It is essential in the production of hemoglobin. Its deficiency may cause diabetes. The sources are soya beans, black gram, carrot, tomato, groundnuts, bajra and barley

Nonnutritive components of diet:

a) Water

b) Roughage
c) Artificial sweeteners
d) Preservatives
e) Plant products

Fiber or roughage has no nutritive value. It is undigested part of the food or it can be said that it cannot be digested by human intestinal tract.It improves intestinal function by adding bulk to the food.

It helps the individual to satisfy the appetite. It prevents constipation.

Eating for weight control :-

A healthy weight is a weight that lowers your risk for health problems, generally Mass Index (BMI) and waist size are good ways to achieve healthy weight.

Methods to calculate BMI = Weight in Kg/(Height in m2)

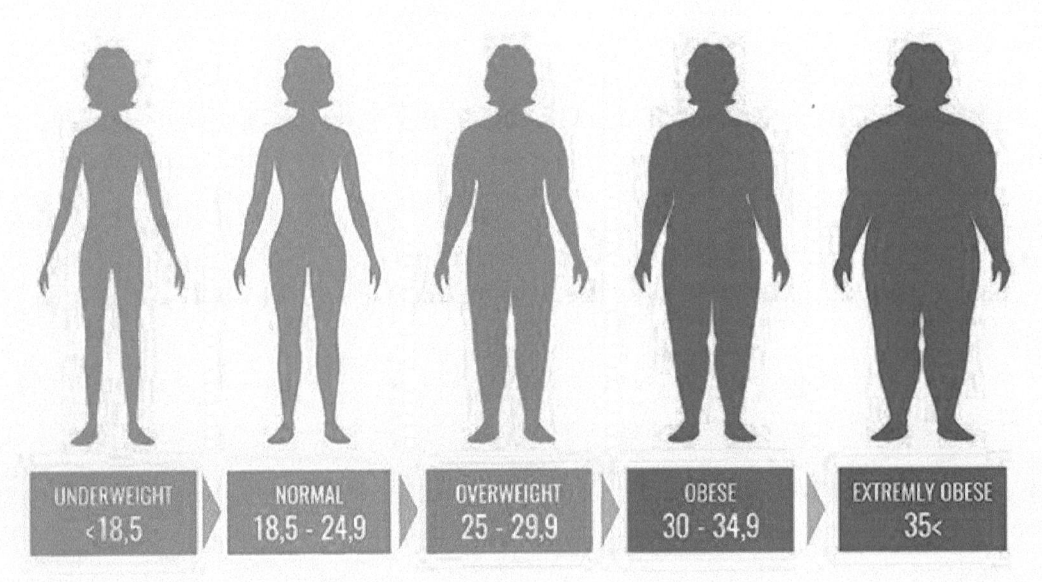

Category of BMI

1. Under Weight
2. Normal Weight
3. Over Weight
4. Obesity Class I
5. Obesity Class II
6. Obesity class III

Here are some useful tips for weight control with proper eating:

a. Avoid common pitfalls
b. Put a stop to emotional eating
c. Tune in what you eat
d. Fill up with fruit, veggies and fiber
e. Indulge without overindulging
f. Take charge of your food environment

PITFALL OF DIETING:

An individual who is overweight wants to reduce weight they starve for reducing weight many times skip meals to lose weight, sometimes take slimming pills.

Extreme Reduction of Calories, Restriction on some nutrients, Skipping meals,Intake of calories through drinking, Intake of Labelled foods, Not preferring physical activities, low energy diet, Taking less liquids
Starving, Under estimating the calories,

Food Intolerance:
Food intolerance is that when a person has difficulty in digesting a particularfood.

Symptoms: Nausea, Vomiting, Pain in joints, headache and rashes on skin, Diarrhea, sweating, palpitations, burning sensations on the skin stomach.

Food Intolerance means the individual elements of certain foods that cannot be properly processed and absorbed by our digestive system

Causes : Absence of activity of enzymes responsible for breaking down the food elements.
These are usually innate sometimes diet related or due to illness.
Food myths:

1. Eggs increases cholesterol level so avoid them
2. Drinking while eating makes you fat
3. Low fat or no fat diet is good.
4. Dieting or Fasting may lose weight.
5. Food eaten late night is more fattening.
6. Low fat milk has less calcium that full fat milk.
7. Vegetarian cannot build muscles.
8. Healthy food is expensive.

CHAPTER SIX

Test and Measurement in Sport

Fitness Test – SAI Khelo India Fitness Test in school :

Age group 5-8 years (Class 1-3) :

At Primary class 1-3, children should acquire Fundamental Movement Skills (FMS) leaving the learning of specific physical activities to later stages. Locomotor, Manipulative & Body Management abilities are key to success in most sports and physical activities.

Abilities of children in class 1-3 which need to be measured and tracked are

1. Body Composition (BMI)
2. Coordination (Plate Tapping)
3. Balance (Flamingo Balance)

1. Body Mass Index (BMI) :

The test performed is Body Mass Index (BMI), which is calculated from body Weight (W) and height(H).

BMI = W / (H x H), where

W = body weight in kilograms and

H = height in meters. The higher the score usually indicating higher levels of body fat.

Body Composition :

It refers primarily to the distribution of muscle and fat in the body. Body size such as height, lengths and girths are also grouped under this component.

2. Plate Tapping Test :

What does it measure :

Tests speed and coordination of limb movement.

Infrastructure/Equipment Required :

Table (adjustable height), 2 yellow discs (20cm diameter), rectangle (30 x 20 cm), stopwatch

How to Perform :

1. If possible, the table height should be adjusted so that the subject is standing comfortably in front of the discs.
2. The two yellow discs are placed with their centres 60 cm apart on the table.
3. The rectangle is placed equidistant between both discs. The nonpreferred hand is placed on the rectangle.
4. The subject moves the preferred hand back and forth between the discs over the hand in the middle as quickly as possible.
5. This action is repeated for 25 full cycles (50 taps).

Scoring: The time taken to complete 25 cycles is recorded

3. Flamingo Balance Test :

What does it measure :

Ability to balance successfully on a single leg. This single leg balance test assesses the strength of the leg, pelvic, and trunk muscle as well as Static balance.

Infrastructure/Equipment Required:

Non Slippery even surface, Stopwatch, can be done on just standing on beam.

How to Perform :

1. Stand on the beam. Keep balance by holding the instructor's hand (if required to start).

2. While balancing on the preferred leg, the free leg is flexed at the knee and the foot of this leg held close to the buttocks

Scoring :

The total number of falls or loss of balance in 60 seconds of balancing is recorded. If there are more than 15 falls in the first 30 seconds, the test is terminated.

Age group 9-18 years (Class 4-12) :

For Class 4 to 12, it is important for students to have an overall physical fitness.

The following Components are to be considered in Physical Health andFitness Profile:

1. BMI,
2. 50mt Speed test,
3. 600mt Run/Walk,
4. Sit & Reach flexibility test,
5. Strength Test (Abdominal Partial Curl Up, Push-Ups for boys, Modified Push- Ups for girls).

2. 50 m Speed Test :

Procedure :

1. Sprint over 50 meters, with the time recorded, start from a stationary standing position.
2. Once the subject is ready, the starter give the instructions "set" then "go" participant should be encouraged to notslow down before crossing the finish line.

Scoring :

Time take to cover 50 m distance is expressed in Seconds.

3. 600 m walk/Run :

Procedure :

1. The subject takes a standing start from the starting line. The subject may walk in between.
2. Objective is to cover the distance in the shortest time when he crosses the finish line he is informed of his time.

4. Sit and Reach Flexibility test :

Procedure :

1. This test involves sitting on the floor with legs stretched out straight ahead.
2.The soles of the feet are placed flat against the box. Both knees should be locked and pressed flat to the floor.
3.The tester may assist by holding them down with the palms facing downwards, and the hands-on top of each other or side by side.

Scoring: The score is recorded to the nearestcentimeter or half inch as the distance reached by the hand.

5. Strength Test - A. Abdominal Partial Curl up :

Procedure :

1. The starting position is lying on the back with the knees flexed and feet 12 inches from the buttocks.
2.The feet cannot be held or rest against on object. The arms are extended and are rested on the thighs. The head is in a neutral position.

Scoring : Record the total number of curl-ups,only, correctly performed curl ups should be counted.

5. Strength Test - B. Push up: For Boys

5. Strength Test – C. Push up [Modified] : For Girls

6.2 Basal Metabolic Rate (BMR) :

The acronym BMR stands for Basal Metabolic Rate. It is the number of calories our body burns during complete rest.We can get an insight into your energy level if you know the BMR levels.

Our body needs some energy even during sleep for performing some basic functions like breathing, circulating blood, and repairing cells.Our body burns more calories by movement and exercise. So, by monitoring our consumption, it will be better to prevent unwanted weight
gains or severe weight loss.

What is the Metabolic Age?

BMR stands for a basal metabolic rate that changes as our age progresses. The peak time for BMR is during teenage and slows down gradually henceforth. As we grow older, consuming fewer calories helps us to keep a better BMR. If your metabolic age is higher, then it is time to exercise to burn off those fats accumulated in your Body.

How to calculate BMR?

BMR was introduced to the world by James Arthur Harris and Francis Gano Benedict. So, the equation is popularly known as the Harris-Benedict formula.

A new equation was formulated in 1990, which is known as the Mifflin-St. George equation.

$P= (10.0 \times m/1\ kg) + (6.25 \times h/1cm) - (5.00 \times a/1\ year) + s$

P= total energy output during rest(BMR)

M= weight of the person in kgs
H= height of the concerned person
A= age of the incumbent
S= constant which is +5 for males and -161 for females

Rikli and Jones -Senior Citizen Test

Rikli and Jones developed the senior citizen fitness test in 2001.
This test has proved to be beneficial for senior citizens.

1. Back Scratch Test :

Purpose :- To assess the upper body (shoulder) flexibility, which is important in performing various jobs such as combing one's hair, putting on overhead garments and reaching for a seat belt etc.

Equipment Required :-
A ruler.
Fingers should be aligned. Measure the distance between the tips of the fingers.
If the finger tips touch then the score is zero.
If they do not touch measure the distance between the fingertips (–ve score).
If they overlap measure by how much (+ive score).

2. Chair Stand Test:

Purpose: The main purpose of this test is to measure the lower body strength, particularly legs strength which is usually required for various tasks such asclimbing stairs, getting in and out of vehicle, bathtub or chair.

Equipments Required:
A chair with a straight back and a seat of at least 44 cm and a stopwatch.

Instructions for Participants :-

1.The participant should sit in the middle of the chair.
2.She/He should keep his hands on the opposite shoulder crossed at the wrists.
3.The feet should be flat on the floor.
4. Her/His back should be erect.
5.Repeat sit up and down for 30 seconds.

Minutes Walk Test :

Purpose : This test measures aerobic fitness of senior citizens.
Equipment required : Measuring tap to mark out the track distances, stopwatch,chairs positioned for resting.

Procedure :

1.The walking course is laid out in a 50 yard (45.72m) rectangular area (dimensions 45 x 5 yards), with cones placed at regular intervals to indicatedistance walked.
2.The aim of this test is to walk as quickly as possible for 6 minutes to cover asmuch distance as possible.
3.Subjects are set their own pace (a preliminary trials is useful to practice pacing), and are able to stop for a rest if they desire.

4. Arm Curl test of Rikli & Jones :

Purpose: It is used to Testing upper body strength of senior citizen
Equipment:Women will curl a 5 lb. weight in this test and men will curl a 8 lbweight for their test.

Procedure :

1.Test assistant will tell to begin and will time for 30 seconds, using thestopwatch or a watch with a second hand.
2.Do as many curls as can in the allotted 30-second time period, moving in acontrolled manner.
3.Do a full curl, squeezing lower arm against upper arm at the top of each curland returning to a straight arm each time. Keep upper arm still.
4. Do not swing the weight.

5. Eight Foot up and Go Test :

Purpose :
To assess speed, agility and balance while moving.These are important inperforming various jobs which require quick

maneuvering, such as getting of abus in time and to answer the phone etc.
Equipments Required:
A chair with straight back (about 44 cm high) a stopwatch, cone marker, measuring tape and an area without any hindrances.

6. Chair sit and reach test :

Purpose : To Test Lower body flexibility. It also plays a role in balance, posture, in fall prevention, or walking. Lower body flexibility is important for maintaining an active, independent lifestyle.
Equipment required :
Ruler, straight back or folding chair, (about 17 inches/ 44 cm high)

CHAPTER SEVEN

PHYSIOLOGY & INJURIES IN SPORT

Physiological factors determining Components of Physical Fitness.

Physiological factors for determining Strength.

1. Muscle size : Bigger and larger muscles can produce more force. Males havelarger muscles than females so the size muscles and strong can with the help ofweight training.

2. Muscle composition: There are two types of fibers in muscles i.e., fast twitch fibers and slow twitch fibers. The muscles which consist of more percentage of fast twitch fibers will produce more strength.

3. Body weight: There is a positive relation between body weight and strength.The individuals who are heavier are stronger than the individuals who are lighterin weight.

Physiological factors determining Flexibility:

1. Muscle strength: - The muscle should have minimum level of strength tomake the movement, especially against the gravity or external force.

2. Joint structure: - There are different types of joint in human body, some ofthe joints intrinsically have greater range of motion than others. For example. The ball and socket joint of the shoulder has the greatest range of motion in comparison to the knee joint

3. Internal environment: -Internal environment of athlete influences the flexibility. For example, warm bath increases body temperature and flexibility whereas 10 minutes outside stay in 10°c temperature reduces the body temperature and flexibility.

4. Injury: -Injuries to connecting tissues and muscles can lead to thickening or fibroin on the affected area. Fibrous tissues are less elastic and can lead to limb shortening and lead to reduce flexibility.

5. Age and gender: - Flexibility decreases with the advancement of age. However, it is trainable. It can be enhanced with the help of training, as strengthand endurance are enhanced. Gender also determines the flexibility. Females tend to be more flexible than male.

6. Active and sedentary life style: -Regular activities enhance the flexibility,whereas inactive individual loses flexibility due to the soft tissues and jointsshrinking and loosing extensibility.

7. Heredity: - Bony structures of joints length and flexibilities of the jointcapsules and surrounding ligaments are genetical and can be altered by stretchingprograms.

Psychological factors for determining speed

1. Explosive strength – For every quick and explosive movement, explosivestrength is indispensable. Like, a quick punch in boxing cannot be delivered ifthe boxer lacks explosive strength. Explosive strength further depends on musclecomposition, muscle size, and muscle coordination.

2. Muscle composition - The muscle which have more fast twitch fibers. Theycan do more speed. The muscle composition is genetically determined. We will improve it only by some training methods.

3. Mobility of nervous system -Motor and sensory nerves of nervouscan be determined by the mobility of nervous system. By training only, we canlimit extent in the mobility of nervous system because speed is determined to agreat extent by genetic factors.

4. Elasticity and Relaxing capacity of muscle –Through the elasticity ofmuscle, muscle can move to a maximum range which reduces the inner hurdlesand is instrumental in speeding up the activity. The muscles which get relaxed soon, they contract easily.

5. Bio-chemical Reserves and Metabolic Power –For doing the exercises which are done quickly muscles need more energy. This energy in our muscles isobtained through the of ATP. The percentage of power and quantity in ATP can be increased through training.

Physiological factors determining endurance:

1.Aerobic capacity: -Aerobic capacity is a measure of the ability of the heart and lungs to get oxygen to the muscles. An example of aerobic capacity is body'sability to take in and use oxygen to improve aerobic performance.

2. Oxygen Uptake: - It is highest rate at which oxygen can be taken up andconsumed by the heart per minute.

3.Cardiac Output: -The cardiac output is simply the amount of blood pumped by the heart per minute.

Effect of exercise on the cardio-respiratory system.

Cardio system –

It consists of three parts: the heart, blood vessels and blood. Its major function is to deliver oxygen and nutrients, remove CO2 and other metabolic waste products, to transport hormones and other molecules, to support thermoregulation and control of body fluid balance and lastly to regulate immune function.

Effect of exercise on the cardio-respiratory system.

The important parts of the respiratory system are the nose, nasal cavity, pharynx,larynx, trachea, bronchi, and lungs. Air can also enter the respiratory system through the oral cavity. Its major functions include, transporting air to the lungs, exchanging gases (O2 and CO2) between the air and blood and regulating blood ph.

Effect of exercise on the cardio-respiratory system.

Increase in heart rate: - When an individual starts exercise, his heart rate increases as per the intensity and duration of exercise.

Increase in stroke volume: -Stroke volume increases proportionally with exercise intensity. It is measured in ml/beat.

Increase in cardiac output: -Cardiac output increases proportionally with theintensity of exercise's is measured in ltr/ minute.

Increases in blood flow: -Cardio-vascular can be distribute more blood to those tissues which have more demand and less blood & those tissues which have less demand for oxygen.

Increase in blood pressure: -During the exercise, systolic blood pressure can increase while diastolic blood pressure usually remains unchanged even during the intensive exercise. Increase in vital air capacity- It is the amount of air which an individual can inhale and exhale with maximum effect. Its capacity varies
from 3500 cc. Due to exercise its capacity increases up to 5500 cc.

Increase in Residual air volume- Due to regular exercise increases the capacity of residual volume from normal capacity.

Passive Alveolus become Active - Regular exercise activates the unused alveoli because much amount of O2 is required in prolonged exercise of daily routine

Effects of exercise on muscular system.

"Muscle is a specialized tissue, which enables the body and its part to move and give shape to the body"

Effects of Exercise

– Change in shape and size of muscle
– More energy supply to muscle Improve in reaction time
– Capillarization
– Reduction fat
– Muscular endurance
– Posture
– Controls extra fat
– Delays fatigue
– Increase food storage
– Strength and speed

Soft tissue refers to tissues that connect, support or surround other structures and organs of the body the muscles, tendons, ligaments, fascial, nerves, fibrous tissue, blood vessels, etc. Soft tissue injuries involve injuries to muscles, ligaments and tendons in the body.

1. Contusion: Muscle injury occurs due to direct hit, with or without any sports equipment. Blood vessels in the muscles are broken, bleeding may occur in the muscles. Stiffness & swelling common sign. Muscle may not respond or may become totally inactive. Common in: Boxing, Wrestling, Kabaddi.
2. Strain: Mild or severe muscle injury. In severe case, muscle may rupture. In case of complete rupture movement of limb is not possible due to severe pain. May happen during practice or clash
3. Sprain (मोच) : May occur due to over stretching or tearing of ligament. Occurs at wrist joint and ankle joint. Sometime fracture is possible along with sprain. Swelling, inflammation, severe pain & tenderness are common symptoms.
4. Abrasion: Skin Injury that Occurs due to friction with any equipment or a fall over the area where the bone is close to skin

5. Bruises (चोट) : An injury appearing as an area of discolored skin (red to blue or dark purple) on the body Caused by a blow or impact rupturing underlying blood vessels.
6. Laceration : Lacerations are wounds that are torn, rather than cut. They have ragged, irregular edges and torn tissue underneath. These wounds are usually made by a blunt, rather than a sharp, object.
7. Incision: A surgical cut made in skin or flesh.

Preventive measures of soft tissue injuries:

1. Proper warming up
2. Proper conditioning of body
3. Scientific equipment & facilities
4. Clean & plain surface of play grounds
5. Knowledge rules & regulation of sports events.
6. Actively & alertness participation during the sports training & competition.
7. Fatigue, sickness & injuries condition to avoid participation in the sports training.

Dislocation:

A dislocation is a separation of two bones where they meet at a joint. Joints are areas where two bones come together.

1. Dislocation of Lower Jaw: Generally, it occurs when the chin strikes to any other object. It may also occur if mouth is opened excessively
2. Dislocation of Shoulder Joint: Dislocation of shoulder joint may occur due to sudden jerk or a fall on hard surface. The end of the hummers comes out from the socket

Types of Bone Fractures:

1. Greenstick fracture: An incomplete fracture in which a bone bends and cracks. This type of fracture usually occurs in children because their bone is soft and flexible.
2. Transverse fracture: A fracture at a right angle to the bone's axis or a straight break right across a bone.
3. Oblique fracture: A fracture is a slanted fracture that occurs when a force is applied diagonally an angle to a bone's long axis.
4. Impacted fracture: It is loss of continuity in the structure of bones.
5. Stress fractures: It is a crack in bone due to high impact physical activity.
6. Comminuted Fracture: A fracture in which the bone fragments.

Prevention from Sports Injuries:

1. Warming up, stretching and cooling down.
2. Undertaking training prior to competition to ensure readiness to play.
3. Including appropriate speed work in training program so muscles are capable of sustaining high acceleration forces.
4. Including appropriate stretching and strengthening exercises in weekly training Programs.

5. Gradually increasing the intensity and duration of training.
6. Maintaining high levels of cardiovascular fitness and muscle endurance to prevent fatigue.
7. Allowing adequate recovery time between workouts or training sessions.
8. Wearing protective equipment, such as shin guards. Mouth guards and helmets.
9. Pre-participation-medical checkup.

P.R.I.C.E Treatment:

The traditional protocol of dealing with sports injury, R.I.C.E., has now been modified to P.R.I.C.E. This refers to the addition of the word "Protection" to Rest, Ice, Compression and Elevation. Protecting the injured area from further damage is crucial to the healing process.

1. Protection:

Protect the affected area from further injury by limiting or avoiding weight bearing through the use of crutches, a cane, or hiking poles. Partially immobilizing the injured area by using a sling, splint, or brace may also be a means of protection.

2. Rest:

Stop using injured part or discontinue activity. It could cause further injury, delay healing, increase pain and stimulate bleeding. Use crutches to avoid bearing weight on injuries of the leg, knee, ankle and foot.

Use splint for injuries of the arm, elbow, wrist and hand

3. Ice:

Ice application contracts blood vessels. Helps stop internal bleeding from injured capillaries and blood vessels. Hastens healing time by reducing swelling around injury.

Keep damp or dry cloth between skin and ice pack. Do not apply ice for longer than 15 to 20 minutes at a time. Apply every hour for 10 to 20 minutes.

4. Compression:

Hastens healing time by reducing swelling around injury.

Decreases seeping of fluid into injured area from adjacent tissues.

Use elasticized bandage, compression sleeve, or cloth.

Wrap injured part firmly.

Do not impair blood supply.

Too tight bandage may cause more swelling.

Wrap over ice.

Loosen the bandage if it gets too tight.

5. Elevation:

Elevate injured part above the level of heart.

Decreases swelling and pain.

Use objects and pillows.

First aid Aim & objectives

First aid: "It is care that is given to an injured or sick person prior to treatment bymedically trained personnel."

Aim of first aid:

The Aim of first aid to save the life of an injured & ill person.

Objectives of first aid:

1. To preserve life
2. To alleviate pain & suffering
3. To prevent the condition from worsening
4. To promote recovery.
5. To procure Early medical Aid.

CHAPTER EIGHT

Biomechanics and Sports

Meaning of Biomechanics

Meaning of Biomechanics:

Bio + Mechanics

Bio = Living organism

Mechanics = Branch of Physical science which deals with force acting on a body in static condition or in moving condition.

Biomechanics: is the study of forces & their effects on human being is moving or in static condition.

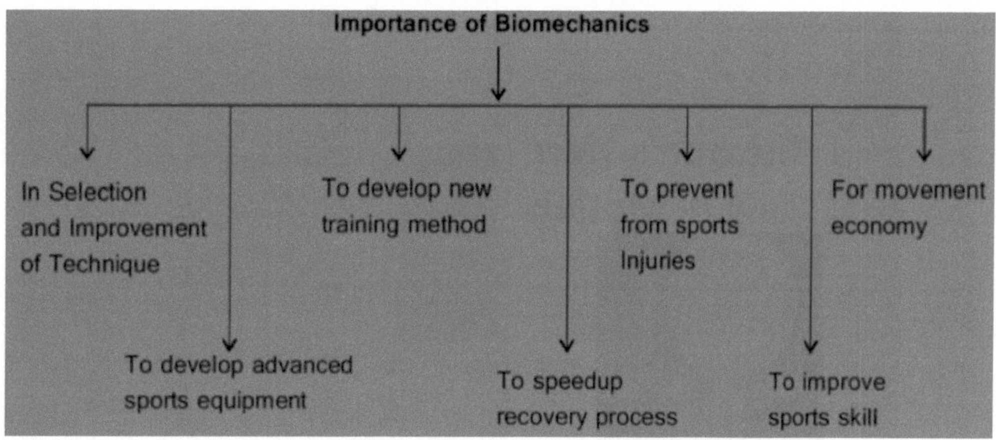

Newton's Laws of motion and their applicationin sports:

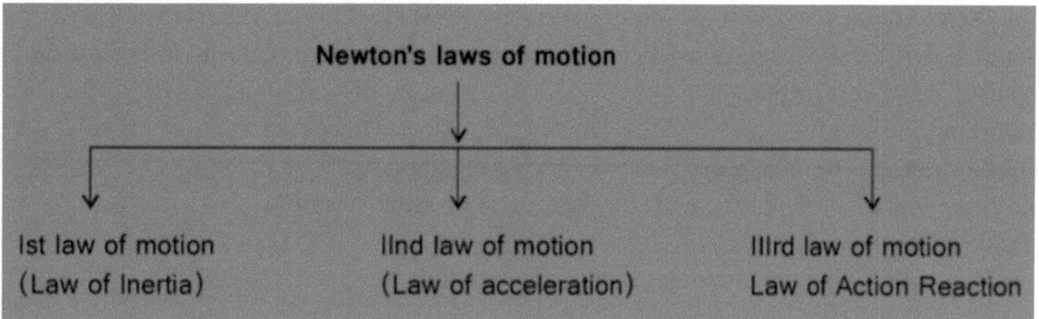

Sir Isaac Newton's three laws of motion describe the motion of massive bodies and how they interact.

Newton published his laws in 1687, in his seminal work "Principia Mathematica"

1st Law of Motion (Law of Inertia):
Any object will be remains in its position until or unless any external force is applied on it.
When a book is placed on a table, it remains stationary in position unless somebody acts to affect it and change its state.
When an object is pushed on the floor, it rolls for a certain distance, then slows down till it stops by the effect of frictional forces between the object and the floor that resist rolling (Friction is an external force that acts to change the object state).
If these forces do not exist, the object would keep moving at a uniform velocity and would not stop.
Newton's First Law is known as the Law of Inertia since the object can change its state of rest or motion by itself.

2nd law of motion (Law of Acceleration):
The rate of change of acceleration is directly proportional to the force applied on the object and inversely proportional to the mass of the object.
F = ma
m = mass
a = acceleration
The second law shows that if you exert the same force on two objects of different mass, you will get different accelerations (changes in motion). The effect (acceleration) on the smaller mass will be greater (more noticeable).

3rd law of motion (Law of action and Reaction):
To Every action, there is equal & opposite reaction

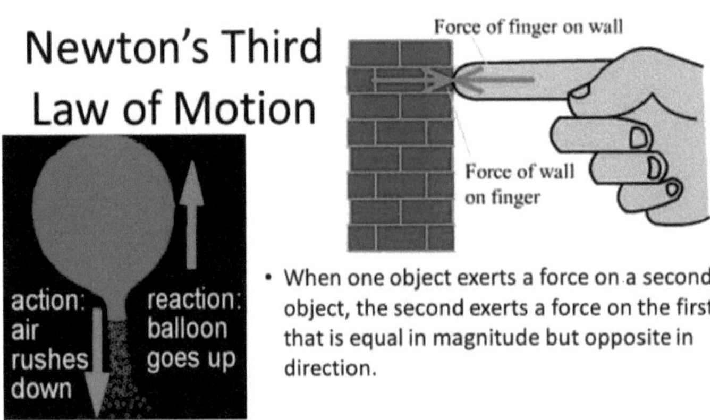

Equilibrium: DYNAMIC AND STATIC & Center of Gravity AND ITS APPLICATION IN SPORTS:

Equilibrium: It is defined as a state of balance or a stable situation, where opposite forces cancel each other out and where no changes are occurring.
Types of Equilibrium
1. Dynamic Equilibrium: It is the balance of the body during movement.
2. Static Equilibrium: It is a balance of the body during its rest or stable position.

Dynamic Equilibrium:
When the body is in equilibrium but continues to move at an unknown speed.
For example,
1. A ball that moves at an unknown speed.
2. Cartwheel in gymnastics

Static Equilibrium:
If the body is in equilibrium when it is stationary, it is called static Equilibrium.

Principles to Determine THE DEGREE OF STABILITY:

1. Broader the base, greater the stability.
2. Lower the center of gravity, higher the stability
3. Body weight is directly proportional to stability.

Centre of gravity:

Centre of gravity is that point in a body or system around which its mass or weight is evenly distributed or balanced and through which the force of gravity acts.

The center of gravity is fixed, provided the size and shape of the body do not change.

Application of Equilibrium

1. In the Starting Blocks, A SPRINTER ' S CENTER OF GRAVITY is

ALIGNED along the rib cage and Forward knee, Thus, maximizing the runner's ability to shoot forward out of the Blocks.

Application of Equilibrium

2. See-Saw

3. Tug of War

Friction & Sports

Friction is the force that opposes the motion of a solid object over another.

There are mainly four types of friction:

1. Static friction,
2. Sliding friction,
3. Rolling friction, and
4. Fluid friction.

Static Friction:

Static friction is defined as the frictional force that acts between the surfaces when they are at rest with respect to each other.

Static Friction Examples:

1. Skiing against the snow
2. Table lamp resting on the table

2. Sliding Friction:

Sliding friction is defined as the resistance that is created between any two objects when they are sliding against each other.

Examples Of Sliding Friction:

1. Sliding of the block across the floor
2. Two cards sliding against each other in a deck

Rolling Friction:

Rolling friction is defined as the force which resists the motion of a ball or wheel and is the weakest types of friction.

Examples Of Rolling Friction:

1. Rolling of the log on the ground
2. Wheels of the moving vehicles

4. Fluid Friction: Fluid friction is defined as the friction that exists between the layers of the fluid when they are moving relative to each other.

Examples Of Fluid Friction:

1. The flow of ink in pens
2. Swimming

Projectile in Sports

What is Projectile?

A projectile is any object thrown into space upon which the only acting force is gravity. The primary force acting on a projectile is gravity. This doesn't necessarily mean that other forces do not act on it, just that their effect is minimal compared to gravity.

The path followed by a projectile is known as a trajectory. A baseball batted or thrown is an example of the projectile.

Factors affecting the flight path of a Projectile are:

1. Gravity.
2. Air Resistance.
3. Speed of Release. (Initial Velocity)
4. Angle of Release
5. Height of Release

Maximum RANGE is Obtained at 45 Degree

CHAPTER NINE

Psychology & Sports

Personality; its definition & types – Trait & Types
The word personality is derived from the Latin word 'Persona', which means 'the mask'.
So, we say that personality is a mask that is used by an individual to deal with the society or the environment.
Personality covers all the physical, mental, social, emotional interest and behavioral qualities of an individual.

"It is the integration of an individual's most characteristicsstructure, mode of behavior, interest, attitudes, capacities,aptitudes, and abilities."

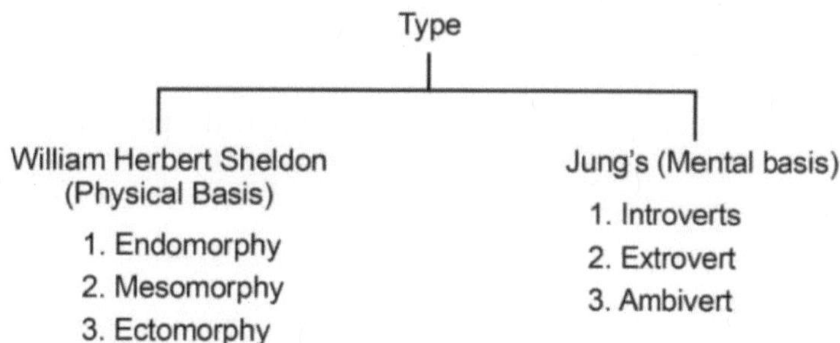

Jung's human personality can be classified into three categories.

1. Introvert: If an individual is motivated or energized by the internal world of thoughts, feelings and reflections is known as Introvert. They are having poor self-confidence, moody, unsocial, quiet and Pessimist.
2. Extrovert: This kind of individual associated with external world of object and other people. They believe in action, social settings, interacting. They are friendly, confident responsive and lively leader.
3. Ambivert: This kind of people have the mix trait of Introvertand Extrovert:

They are having few Friends.

Big five personality theory

1. Openness
2. Conscientiousness
3. Extraversion
4. Agreeableness
5. Neuroticism

1. **Opnness**	2. **Conscientiousness**	3. **Extraversion**
Social	Self discipline	Energetic
Imaginative	Dedicated	Positivenees
Interest	Hard worker	Accepting nature
Curiousity	Aspirant	Social
Creativity		Talkative
Emotional		Friendly

4. **Agreeableness**	5. **Neuroticism**
Cooperative	Angryness
Managed	depression
Soft hearted.	worried

1.Openness Traits: The assessment of openness traits shows that how the person is

- Imaginative
- Insightful
- Having variety of interest
- With degree of intellectual curiosity
- Creative
- Able to enjoy the new experiences
- Able to learn new changes & Concept

2. Conscientiousness: The assessment of this trait shows that how the person is able to

- Compete with life challenges
- Self disciplined
- Act dutifully
- Plan & Organize
- Work independently
- Do hard work

3. Extraversion:

The assessment of this trait shows that how the person.

- Is energetic
- Has positive emotions
- Has Assertiveness
- Is sociable
- Is talkative
- Is fun loving
- Has friendly nature or has tendency to make new friends
- Able to get affection from other

4. Agreeableness:

The assessment of this trait shows that how the person.

- Has sense of cooperation

- Is systematic
- Is kind
- Is friendly
- Is gentle

5. Neuroticism:

The assessment of this trait shows. How the person.

- Has emotional stability
- Is able to control anger
- Is able to controlthe level of anxiety

Aggression:

It is a physical or verbal behavior which is directed towards the goal of harming other living being either physically or psychologically.

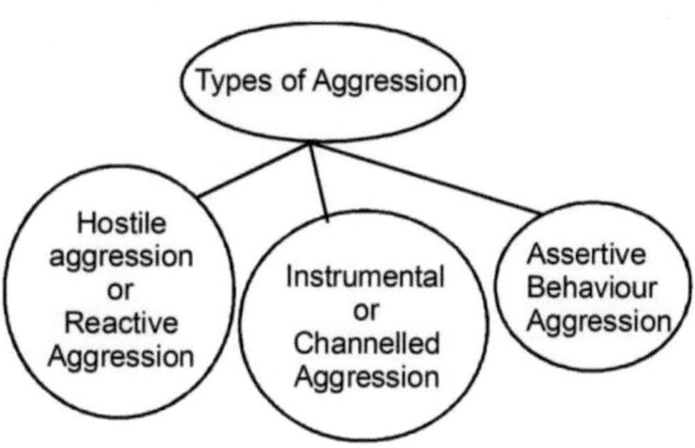

Hostile Agression:	**Instrumental Aggression**	**Assertive Behaviour**
(Reactive aggression)	(channelled aggression)	1. Legitimate force
1. To cause harm	1. To win comp.	2. Psychological discomfort
2. Physical or psychological	2. Without actual anger	3. Eg: sledging
3. Eg: Delibrate bouncer in cricket	3. Eg:Aggressive tackle in football	

Psychological Attributes in Sports

Self-esteem :

It is how we value and perceive ourselves. It's based on our opinions and beliefsabout ourselves.

We might also think of this as self-confidence.

Mental Imagery:

It is the representation of things in mind that are not currently being sensed by sense organs.

Common examples of mental images include daydreaming Another is of the pictures seen by athletes during training or before a competition, outlining each step they will take to accomplish their goal.

Self-Talk:

Self-talk is the way you talk to yourself, or your inner voice.

Goal Setting:

Goal setting involves the development of an action plan designed in order to motivate and guide a person or group toward a goal

CHAPTER TEN

Training in sports

Concept of Talent Identification and Talent Development in Sports

Talent Identification is essential to ensure that the appropriate players are being selected. A selection must be made fairly and equitably. This demands a better understanding of player identification and adopting a suitable selection policy.

Talent identification:

It is the method of recognizing current players that have the potential to excel. It involves an attempt to predict an individual's future capacity for performance. It is based on:

1. Physical attributes and Physiological skills,
2. Technical skills,
3. Psychological skills,
4. Cognitive skills, and
5. Social skills.

Talent Development:

It is the method of providing athletes with a suitable learning environment so as build and retain strategically important skills among players.

Key Factors:

1. Physical Factors
2. Physiological Factors
3. Sociological Factors
4. Psychological Factors
5. Obstacles

Introduction to Sports Training Cycle – Micro, Meso, Macro Cycle.

A training plan is constructed by incorporating various training cycles.

These cycles are:

1. Micro,
2. Meso and
3. Macro;

where Micro is the shortest cycle which may last for 3-10 days. Meso cycle is the medium duration cycle and may be done for 3-6 weeks. Lastly, Macro cycle, this is the longest duration cycle that lasts up to 12 months or a year. A macro cycle consists of different micro and mesocycles.

Types & Method to Develop – Strength, Endurance and Speed

1. Strength

It is the ability to act or to overcome the resistance.

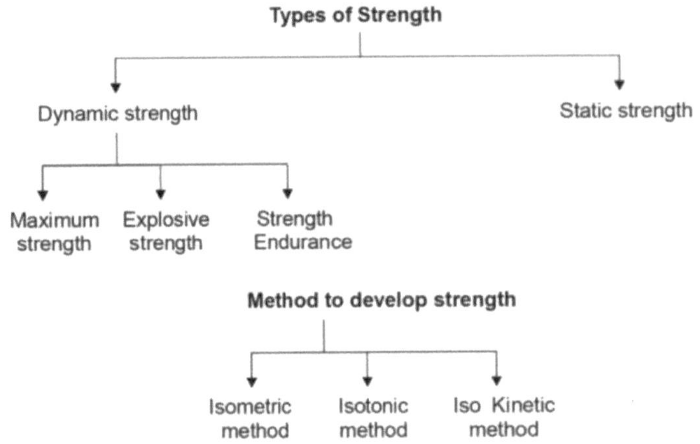

The following are its types:

(a) Maximum strength: -

Ability to act as against maximum resistance

(b) Explosive strength:

Ability to act against resistance withSpeed.

Ex: Take-off in Long jump

(c) Strength Endurance: Ability to act against resistance under condition of fatigue.

Following mention methods are used to improve strength:

1. Isometric Exercise:

The word Isometric is comprised of 2 words "Iso", "same" and "metric", "length".

Means when we do these exercises work done cannot be observed.

These exercises require less time and equipment's and can be carried out anywhere.

These exercises are useful for maintaining strength in case of injury.

Eg : Archery, Weight lifting, Gymnastic are the examples of Isometric movements.

Work done = Force X Distance moved but distance moved is 0, therefore, work done is zero.

2. Isotonic Exercises: -

"Iso" Means 'same' and 'tonic' means tone.

In these types of exercise when we do movements it can be observed directly. The length of muscles can be seen and called eccentric contraction andconcentric contraction accordingly.

Example: When we throw a ball, jump, run, weight training, Jumping on the spot

If muscle contract and changes its length to produce force, the contraction type is Isotonic.

These increase the length of the muscles and are good forconditioning in sports.

3. Iso-Kinetic Exercises:

"Iso" - 'Same' "and' kinetic - motion'.

These exercises were introduced by J.J. perrine in 1968. These exercises are done by specially design machine and are combination of Isotonic and Iso-metric exercises.

2. Endurance

It is ability to continue the activity under the condition of fatigue or for a long time.

Or

the capacity of something to last or to withstand wear and tear.

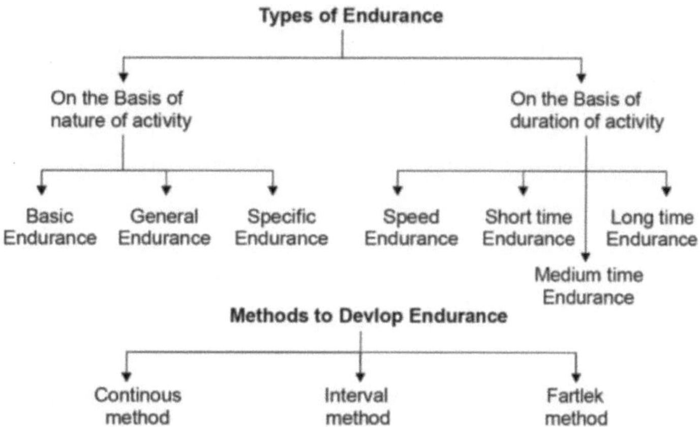

Types of endurance:

On the Basis of nature of activity:

1. Basic Endurance: -

It is the ability of an Individual to do the movement in which large no. of body and muscles involve at slow pace for a duration such as Walking, Jogging, Swimming at a moderate speed.

2. General Endurance: -

It is the ability of an individual to resist fatigue satisfactorily caused by different type of activities.

3. Specific Endurance: -

It is the ability of an individual to complete the task without any fatigue. Its requirement depends upon the nature of activity (Games and Sports) requirement of specific endurance of a boxer is different from that of a wrestler.

On the Basis of duration of activity:

1. Speed Endurance: -

It is the ability of an individual to perform a movement with high speed to resist of fatigue in activities upto 45 seconds.

2. Short term endurance: -

Short term endurance is needed to resist fatigue in sports activities lasting from 45 seconds to 2 minutes.

Ex. 800 m race.

3. The medium-term endurance: -

It is the activity lasting from 2.min to 11 minutes. Ex. 1500 & 3000 mts.

4. Long term Endurance: -

It is needed for those sports which require more than 11 minutes time.

Ex. 5000m to 1000m cross country race.

1. Continuous Method: -

In continuous of method, the exercise is done for a long duration without taking rest. We do the exercise for a long duration. So, the intensity of work is low. The heart rate during the exercise for a sportsman should be between 140-160 beats per minutes. Its duration of exercise should be more than 30 minutes.

Ex. running walking, cycling, cross-country race etc.

2. Interval Method: -

This method is very effective for developing endurance for track runners. Intervals are given to the athlete in between the repetition for recovery.

The Heart should go up to 180 beat/ min. and when the heart rate comes down to 120-130 beats/ min again the repetition/ work starts. The training load should be given again after checking the heart rate of the athlete. Ex. Middle distance race, football, hockey etc.

Fartlek Training Method:

This method was developed by Swedish coach "Gosta Holmer" in 1930 in Sweden. So, it is also known as "Swedish play" or "Speed play" (charges his/her pace.

Athlete changes his/her speed according. So, it is self-disciplined in nature. The heart rate fluctuates between 140 -180 beats/ minute. Fartlek training involves varying our pace throughout our run. Alternating between fast and slow pace.

3. Speed

It is the ability to do movement as quick as possible.

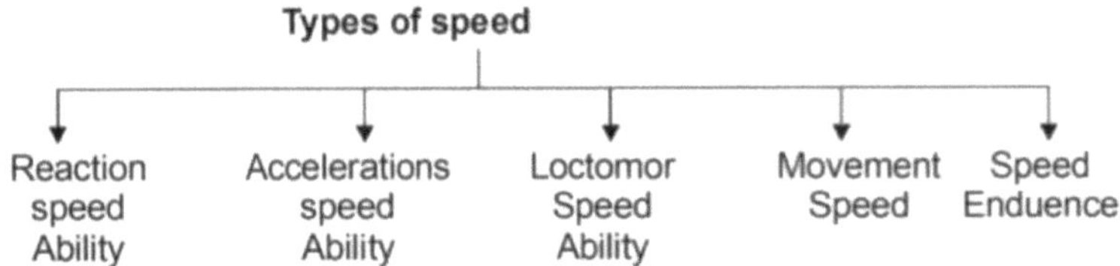

Types of speed Ability:

1. Reaction speed ability: It is the ability to act against a signal.
2. Acceleration speed ability: It is the ability to achieve maxspeed in minimum possible time.
3. Movement speed ability: It is the ability to do a single small movement in minimum possible time.
4. Locomotor speed ability: It is the ability to maintain maxspeed as long as possible.
5. Speed Endurance : It is the ability to do the movement asquick as possible under the condition of fatigue.

Pace run:

Pace run means running the whole distance with a constant speed. Generally, 800 meter and above races are included in pace races. An athlete must conserve his energy by reducing the speed.

Acceleration Run:

Acceleration run are usually used to develop speed indirectly by improving explosive strength, technique, flexibility and movement frequency. It is the ability of a sprinter to achieve high speed from a stationary position. Sufficient intervals should be provided between the repetitions.

Types & Method to Develop – Flexibility and Coordinative Ability

Flexibility:

Flexibility is the range of movement of the joint of a sports person.

Methods to develop Flexibility:

1.Slow Stretch and hold method: We stretch our joint to maximum limit and hold it for a few seconds before returning to the initial Phase. The holding period must be not more than 3 to 8 sec. The method is also use for improving passive flexibility

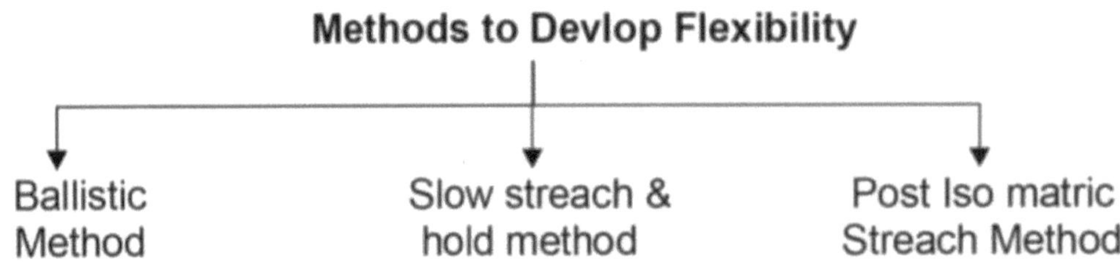

2. Ballistic Method –

In this method the stretching exercises are done in a swing, so this is called the ballistic method. A proper warm - up should be done before this exercise. Stretching of the muscle can be done in a rhythm.

Post - Isometric Stretch Method –

PNF stretching is currently the fastest and most effective way known to increase static passive flexibility.

PNF is an acronym for Proprioceptive Neuromuscular Facilitation. It is not really a type of stretching but is a technique of combining passive stretching and isometric stretching in order to achieve maximum static flexibility After assuming an initial passive stretch, the muscle being stretched is isometrically contracted for 7-15 seconds, after which the muscle is briefly relaxed for 2-3 seconds, and then immediately subjected to a passive stretch which stretches the muscle even further than the initial passive stretch. This final passive stretch is held for 10-15 seconds. The muscle is then relaxed for 20 seconds before performing another PNF technique.

Co-ordinative abilities:

Coordinative abilities mainly depend on the central nervous system.

The coordinative abilities are those abilities of an individual which enable the individual to do various related activities properly as well as efficiently.Our accuracy, rhythm, flow and constancy depend on our coordinative abilities.

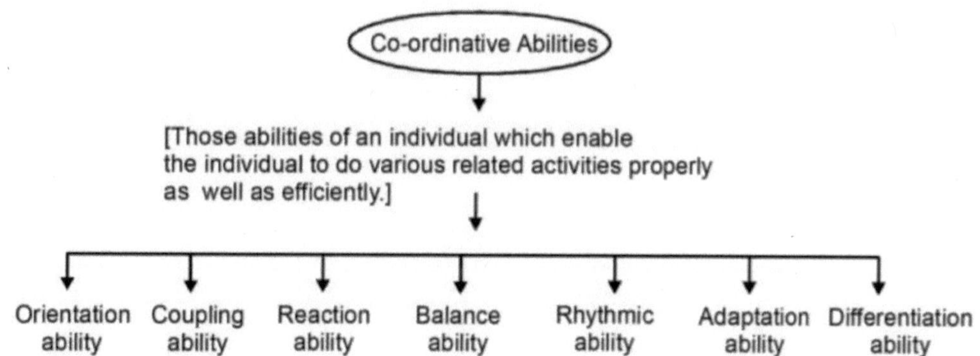

Printed by Libri Plureos GmbH in Hamburg,
Germany